COMPLETE YOUR
RESISTANCE LIBRARY

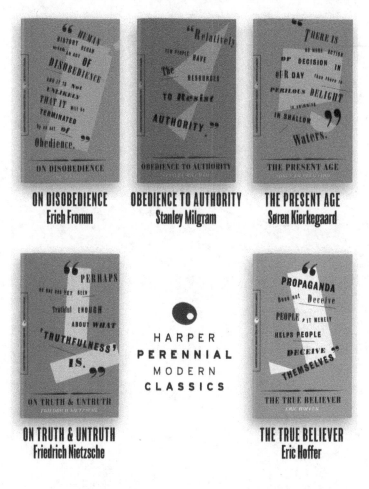

ON DISOBEDIENCE
Erich Fromm

OBEDIENCE TO AUTHORITY
Stanley Milgram

THE PRESENT AGE
Søren Kierkegaard

**HARPER
PERENNIAL
MODERN
CLASSICS**

ON TRUTH & UNTRUTH
Friedrich Nietzsche

THE TRUE BELIEVER
Eric Hoffer

Available in Paperback

About the Translator

TAYLOR CARMAN is Professor of Philosophy at Barnard College in New York City. He is the author of *Heidegger's Analytic* and *Merleau-Ponty* and coeditor of *The Cambridge Companion to Merleau-Ponty*.

ON TRUTH
AND UNTRUTH

Selected Writings

Friedrich Nietzsche

Translated and Edited by

TAYLOR CARMAN

The Resistance Library

HARPER**PERENNIAL** ✖ MODERN**THOUGHT**

NEW YORK • LONDON • TORONTO • SYDNEY • NEW DELHI • AUCKLAND

FIRST HARPER PERENNIAL MODERN THOUGHT EDITION PUB-LISHED 2010.
FIRST HARPER PERENNIAL RESISTANCE LIBRARY EDITION PUB-LISHED 2019.

Designed by Justin Dodd

Library of Congress Cataloging-in-Publication Data is available upon request.

ISBN 978-0-06-293084-2 (pbk.)

23 24 25 26 27 LBC 10 9 8 7 6

Contents

Translator's Note

This book contains a small sample of Nietzsche's published and unpublished writings on the nature and value of truth. They all have appeared in various English editions before, though never in a single volume. I have benefitted greatly from comparing those earlier translations both to one another and to my own. My selection of texts is bound to be both incomplete and somewhat arbitrary. I have tried to include what strike me as some of Nietzsche's most memorable and important pronouncements on truth, truthfulness, and untruth. But of

course there are many others, no doubt equally worthy, throughout his entire corpus. I have arranged the texts in (roughly) chronological sequence to give the reader some sense of how, as it seems to me, his views on truth shifted, evolved, and eventually became deeper, subtler, and more sophisticated with the passage of time. Like his critique of morality, Nietzsche's anxiety about truth progressed from skeptical doubt about its attainability, even its intelligibility, to arguably more profound and original questions concerning its value: Is truth *good*? Why? The "will to truth" is real. Is it *desirable*?

Nietzsche made frequent use of ellipsis as a stylistic device; it indicates (something like) a dramatic pause, not omission. In two cases I have indicated omissions of my own with ellipses in brackets.

—Taylor Carman

1

On the Pathos of Truth
(1872)

Is fame really just the most delicious morsel of our self-love? It has, after all, attached itself to the most uncommon men, as an ambition, and in turn to their most uncommon moments. These are moments of sudden illumination in which man stretches out a commanding arm, as if creating a world, light shining forth and spreading out around him. He is then filled with the deeply gratifying certainty that what

enraptured and exalted him into the farthest regions, the height of this *one* sensation, can never be denied to posterity; in the eternal necessity of this rare illumination for all those to come man sees the necessity of his fame. Far into the future, mankind needs him, and just as that moment of illumination is the embodiment and epitome of his innermost essence, so, too, he believes himself, as the man of this moment, to be immortal, dismissing all others as dross, rot, vanity, brutishness, or pleonasm, leaving them to perish.

We view all disappearance and demise with discontent, often with astonishment, as if we experienced in it something at bottom impossible. We are disturbed when a tall tree breaks, and a crumbling mountain aggrieves us. Every New Year's Eve, we feel the mystery of the contradiction of being and becoming. What offends moral man above all, though, is that an instant of supreme universal perfection should

vanish without a trace, like a falling star, leaving nothing to posterity. His imperative reads instead: whatever *once* served more beautifully to propagate the concept "man" must continue to exist forever. That all the great moments form a chain; that, like mountain peaks, they unite mankind across the millennia; that the greatest things from a bygone age are also great for me; and that the prescient faith of the lust for fame will be fulfilled—that is the idea at the very foundation of *culture*.

The terrible struggle of culture is ignited by the demand that what is great should be eternal; for everything else that continues to live cries out, No! The customary, the small, the common fills every nook and cranny of the world like an oppressive atmosphere we are all condemned to breathe, smoldering around what is great; hindering, choking, suffocating, deadening, smothering, dimming, deluding, it throws itself onto the road the great must travel on the way to im-

mortality. The road goes through human brains! Through the brains of pitiful, short-lived creatures who, given over to their cramped needs, rise again and again to the same afflictions and, with great effort, manage to fend off ruin for a short time. They want to live, to live a bit—at any price. Who would discern among them that arduous torch race that only the great survive? And yet time and again some awaken who, seeing what is great, feel inspired, as if human life were a glorious thing, and as if the most beautiful fruit of this bitter plant were the assurance that someone once walked proudly and stoically through this existence, another with deep thoughts, a third with mercy, but all of them leaving behind a *single* lesson: that he who lives life most beautifully is he who does not hold it in great esteem. But while the common man regards this bit of existence with such morbid seriousness, those on their journey to immortality knew how to respond to it with an Olympian

laugh, or at least with sublime disdain; often they went to their graves with irony—for what did they have to bury?

The boldest knights among those addicted to glory, those who believe they will find their coat of arms hanging on a constellation, must be sought among the *philosophers*. They address their efforts not to a "public," to the agitation of the masses and the cheering applause of their contemporaries; it is in their nature to travel the road alone. Their talent is the rarest and, in a certain respect, the most unnatural in nature, shutting itself off from and hostile even to kindred talents. The wall of their self-sufficiency must be hard as diamond not to be shattered and destroyed, for everything is on the move against them, man and nature. Their journey to immortality is more arduous and impeded than any other, and yet no one can be as sure as the philosopher about reaching his goal, since he knows not where to stand, if not on the wings

of all ages; for a disregard of the present and the momentary is of the nature of philosophical contemplation. He has the truth; let the wheel of time roll where it will, it can never escape the truth.

It is important to realize that such men did indeed once live. One could never imagine as a mere idle possibility the pride of the wise Heraclitus,* who may serve as our example. For all striving for knowledge seems in itself unsatisfied and unsatisfying, which is why, without having learned it from history, one could hardly believe in such regal self-esteem, such boundless confidence in being the one lucky suitor of truth. Such men live in their own solar system; that is where one must look for them. Even a Pythagoras, an Empedocles treated himself with a superhuman esteem, indeed with an almost religious awe, though the bond of compassion, to-

---

* Greek Presocratic philosopher, active around 500 B.C.E.

gether with grand faith in the transmigration of souls and the unity of all living things, led them back again to other men, and to their salvation. Only in the most rugged mountain wasteland, however, can one get a chilling sense of the feeling of solitude that pervaded the recluse of the Ephesian temple of Artemis.* No overwhelming feeling of sympathetic excitement, no craving, no desire to help or to save emanates from him—he is like a shining planet without an atmosphere. His eye, fiery and turned inward, looks lifeless and cold from without, as if just for the sake of appearance. All around him, waves of delusion and distortion crash onto the fortress of his pride; he turns away in disgust. Yet even people with tender hearts shun such a tragic mask; in some remote sanctuary, amid the images of gods, in cold, magnificent archi-

---

* A native of the ancient Ionian city of Ephesus on the Greek-inhabited coast of Asia Minor, Heraclitus is said to have written a single book, which he deposited in the temple of Artemis.

tecture, such a figure might seem more intelligible. Among men, as a man, Heraclitus was
an enigma; and when he was seen watching
the games of shouting children, he was ponder-
ing what no mortal ever pondered on such an
occasion: the game of the great cosmic child,
Zeus, and the eternal sport of world destruction
and world creation.* He had no need of men,
not even for his knowledge; he cared not at all
for what one could learn from them, nor what
other sages before him were at pains to discover.
"I searched out myself," he said, using a word
that refers to the fathoming of an oracle: as if
he and no one else were the true embodiment
and achievement of the Delphic maxim "Know
yourself."

What he heard in this oracle, however, he
took to be immortal wisdom, eternally worthy

---

* "Lifetime [or eternity] is a child at play, moving pieces in a
game. Kingship belongs to the child." Charles H. Kahn, *The Art
and Thought of Heraclitus* (Cambridge University Press, 1981), 71.

of interpretation, in the same sense in which the prophetic utterances of the sibyl are immortal. It is sufficient for the most distant generations; may they interpret it simply as the saying of an oracle, just as he himself, like a Delphic god, "neither speaks nor conceals."* Although he pronounces it "without laughter, without ornaments and scented ointments" but rather "frothing at the mouth," it *must* resound thousands of years into the future.† For the world always needs truth, and so will always need Heraclitus, though he does not need it. What is fame to *him*! "Fame among constantly fleeting mortals!" as he scornfully exclaims.‡ That's something for singers and

---

* "The Lord [i.e., Apollo] whose oracle is in Delphi neither declares nor conceals, but gives a sign." *The Art and Thought of Heraclitus*, 42.

† "The Sibyl with raving mouth utters things mirthless and unadorned and unperfumed, and her voice carries through a thousand years because of the god who speaks through her." *The Art and Thought of Heraclitus*, 45.

‡ "The best choose one thing in exchange for all, everflowing fame among mortals; but most men have sated themselves like

poets, and for those before him who were known as "wise" men—let them gulp down the most delicious morsels of their self-love; the stuff is too common for him. His fame matters to men, not to him; his self-love is the love of truth—and this very truth tells him that the immortality of man needs him, not that he needs the immortality of the man Heraclitus.

Truth! Rapturous delusion of a god! What does truth matter to human beings!

And what was the Heraclitean "truth"!

And where has it gone? A vanished dream, wiped from the faces of men, along with other dreams!— It was not the first!

Of all that we with such proud metaphors call "world history" and "truth" and "fame," a heartless demon might have nothing to say but this:

---

cattle." *The Art and Thought of Heraclitus*, 73. Contrary to Nietzsche's reading, the scorn in this fragment is aimed not at seekers of fame but at the bovine herd.

"In some remote corner of the sprawling universe, twinkling among the countless solar systems, there was once a star on which some clever animals invented *knowledge*. It was the most arrogant, most mendacious minute in world history, but it was only a minute. After nature caught its breath a little, the star froze, and the clever animals had to die. And it was time, too: for although they boasted of how much they had come to know, in the end they realized they had gotten it all wrong. They died and in dying cursed truth. Such was the species of doubting animal that had invented knowledge."

This would be man's fate were he nothing more than a thinking animal; truth would drive him to despair and annihilation, truth eternally damned to be untruth. All that is proper to man, however, is faith in the attainable truth, in the ever approaching, confidence-inspiring illusion. Does he not in fact live *by* constant deception? Doesn't nature conceal virtually

everything from him, even what is nearest, for example, his own body, of which he has only a spurious "consciousness"? He is locked up in this consciousness, and nature has thrown away the key. O fateful curiosity of the philosopher, who longs to peer out just once through a crack in the chamber of consciousness—perhaps then he gains an intimation that man rests in the indifference of his ignorance on the greedy, the insatiable, the disgusting, the merciless, the murderous, suspended in dreams on the back of a tiger.

"Let him hang," cries *art*. "Wake him up," cries the philosopher, in the pathos of truth. Yet, even as he believes himself to be shaking the sleeper, he himself sinks into a still deeper magical slumber—perhaps then he dreams of "ideas" or of immortality. Art is mightier than knowledge, for *it* wants life, and knowledge attains as its ultimate end only—annihilation.

2

On Truth and Lie
in a Nonmoral Sense
(1873)

1

In some remote corner of the sprawling universe, twinkling among the countless solar systems, there was once a star on which some clever animals invented *knowledge*. It was the most arrogant, most mendacious minute in "world history," but it was only a minute. After nature caught its breath a little, the star froze,

and the clever animals had to die.—One could invent a fable like this and still not have illustrated sufficiently how miserable, how shadowy and fleeting, how aimless and arbitrary the human intellect appears in nature. There were eternities in which it did not exist, and when it has vanished once again, it will have left nothing in its wake. For the human intellect has no further task beyond human life. Instead, it is merely human, and only its owner and producer regards it so pathetically as to suppose that it contains in itself the hinge on which the world turns. If we could communicate with a mosquito, we would learn that it, too, flies through the air with this same pathos, feeling itself to be the moving center of the entire world. There is nothing in nature so abject and lowly that it would not instantly swell up like a balloon at the faintest breath of that cognitive faculty. And just as every baggage carrier wants admirers, so, too, the

proudest man of all, the philosopher, thinks he sees the eyes of the universe trained from all sides telescopically on his thoughts and his deeds.

It is remarkable that the intellect manages this, considering it is simply an expedient supplied to the unluckiest, the most delicate, the most transitory creatures in order to detain them for a minute in existence; from which, without that added extra, they would have every reason to flee as swiftly as Lessing's son.* The arrogance involved in cognition and sensation, spreading a blinding fog over men's eyes and senses, deceives them

---

* The German dramatist Gotthold Ephraim Lessing (1729–1781) wrote of his stillborn child, "And I was so sorry to lose him, this son! For he had so much good sense, so much good sense! . . . Was it not good sense [on his part] that they had to pull him into the world with iron forceps? That he was so quick to recognize the rubbish? — Was it not good sense that he seized the first opportunity to get away again?" Letter to Johann Joachim Eschenburg, 31 December 1777. *Lessings Briefe in einem Band* (Berlin und Weimar: Aufbau-Verlag, 1967), 411.

about the value of existence by implying the most flattering evaluation of cognition. Its most general effect is deception—but even its most particular effects have something of the same quality.

The intellect, as a means of preserving the individual, develops its principal strengths in dissimulation, for this is the means by which weaker, less robust individuals preserve themselves, it being denied to them to wage the battle of existence with the horns or sharp fangs of a beast of prey. This art of dissimulation reaches its peak in man: here deception, flattery, lying and cheating, talking behind the backs of others, keeping up appearances, living in borrowed splendor, donning masks, the shroud of convention, playacting before others and before oneself—in short, the continual fluttering around the flame of vanity is so much the rule and the law that virtually nothing is as incomprehensible as how

an honest and pure drive to truth could have arisen among men. They are deeply immersed in illusions and dream images; their eyes glide only over the surface of things and see "forms"; their sensations nowhere lead to truth but content themselves with registering stimuli and playing a touching-feeling game, as it were, on the back of things. What is more, man lets his dreams lie to him at night, his whole life long, his moral sense never trying to prevent it; whereas they say there are people who have managed to quit snoring by sheer willpower. What does man actually know of himself? Could he ever be capable, even just once, of perceiving himself entire, laid out as if in a glass case? Does nature not conceal virtually everything from him, even his body, banishing and locking him up in a proud, spurious consciousness, far removed from the convolutions of the bowels, the rapid flow of the bloodstream, the intricate vibrations of nerve fibers?

Nature has thrown away the key; and woe unto that fateful curiosity that might once manage to peer out through a crack in the chamber of consciousness and gain an intimation that man rests in the indifference of his ignorance on the merciless, the greedy, the insatiable, the murderous, suspended in dreams on the back of a tiger. Where in the world, given this setting, can the drive to truth ever have come from?

In the natural state of things, the individual, inasmuch as he wants to protect himself against other individuals, uses his intellect mostly for dissimulation. But because, out of both necessity and boredom, he wants to exist socially and in herds, man needs a peace treaty and strives at the least to rid his world of the crudest forms of *bellum omnium contra omnes*.* This peace treaty, however, brings with it

---

* "War of all against all": Thomas Hobbes's description of the state of nature.

something like the first step in the attainment of that enigmatic drive to truth. Namely, what is henceforth to count as "truth" is now fixed, that is, a uniformly valid and binding designation of things is invented, and the legislation of language likewise yields the first laws of truth. For here a distinction is drawn for the first time between truth and lie: the liar uses valid designations—words—to make the unreal appear real; he says, for instance, "I am rich," precisely when the proper designation for his condition would be "poor." He misuses fixed conventions by various substitutions or even inversions of names. If he does this in self-serving or otherwise injurious ways, society will no longer trust him and will therefore exclude him from its ranks. So it is that men flee not so much from being cheated as from being harmed by cheating. Even on this level, it is at bottom not deception they hate but the dire, inimical consequences of certain kinds of deception. So,

too, only to a limited extent does man want truth. He desires the pleasant, life-preserving consequences of truth; to pure knowledge without consequences he is indifferent, to potentially harmful and destructive truths he is even hostile. And besides, what is the status of those linguistic conventions? Are they perhaps products of knowledge, of our sense for truth? Do the designations and the things coincide? Is language the full and adequate expression of all realities?

Only through forgetfulness can man ever come to imagine that he possesses truth to that degree. If he does not wish to rest content with truth in the form of a tautology, that is, with empty husks, he will forever be passing illusions off as truths. What is a word? The copy of a nerve stimulus in sounds. To go on to infer from the nerve stimulus to a cause outside us, however, is already the result of a false and unjustified application of the principle of suffi-

cient reason. If truth alone had been decisive in the genesis of language, and the standpoint of certainty in the genesis of the designations of things, how would we be entitled to say, "The stone is hard," as if "hard" were something otherwise known to us and not a wholly subjective impression? We divide things according to genders: we call the tree (*der Baum*) masculine, the plant (*die Pflanze*) feminine—what arbitrary transferences! How far-flung beyond the canon of certainty! We speak of a snake: the designation pertains only to its slithering movement and so could as easily apply to a worm. What arbitrary demarcations, what one-sided preferences for now this, now that property of a thing! All the different languages, set alongside one another, show that when it comes to words, truth—full and adequate expression—is never what matters; otherwise there wouldn't be so many languages. The "thing in itself" (which would be, precisely, pure truth without

consequences) is utterly unintelligible, even for the creator of a language, and certainly nothing to strive for, for he designates only the relations of things to human beings and helps himself to the boldest metaphors. First, to transfer a nerve stimulus into an image—first metaphor! The image again copied in a sound—second metaphor! And each time a complete leap out of one sphere into an entirely new and different one. One can imagine someone profoundly deaf who has never had any sensation of tone or of music: just as he will gaze in amazement at Chladnian sound figures in sand,* will find their causes in the vibration of the strings, and will swear that he now surely knows what people call a tone—so it is for all of us when it comes to language. We think we know something about the things themselves when we

---

* The German physicist and musician Ernst Chladni (1756–1827) invented a technique showing patterns of vibration in sand on glass plates.

speak of trees, colors, snow, and flowers, yet we possess only metaphors of the things, which in no way correspond to the original essences. Just as the tone appears as a shape in the sand, so, too, the enigmatic X of the thing in itself appears first as nerve stimulus, then as image, finally as sound. In any case, the emergence of language did not come about logically, and the very material in which and with which the man of truth—the scientist, the philosopher—later works and builds derives, if not from Cloud Cuckoo Land, then at least not from the essence of things either.

Let us contemplate in particular the formation of concepts: every word becomes a concept, not just when it is meant to serve as a kind of reminder of the single, absolutely individualized original experience to which it owes its emergence, but when it has to fit countless more or less similar—that is, strictly speaking, never equal, hence blatantly unequal—cases.

Every concept arises by means of the equating of the unequal. Just as certain as it is that no one leaf is exactly the same as any other, so, too, it is certain that the concept *leaf* is formed by arbitrarily ignoring these individual differences, by forgetting what distinguishes one from the other, thus giving rise to the notion that there is in nature something other than leaves, something like "The Leaf," a kind of prototype according to which all leaves were woven, drawn, delineated, colored, crimped, painted, but by unskilled hands, so that no specimen turned out correctly or reliably as a true copy of the prototype. We call a man honest. We ask, "Why did he act so honestly today?" Our answer is, usually, "Because of his honesty." Honesty! Which is again like saying, "Leaf is the cause of leaves." We really have no knowledge at all of an essential quality called Honesty, but we do know countless individualized, hence unequal, actions, which we equate

by leaving aside the unequal and henceforth designate as honest actions; finally, from them we formulate a *qualitas occulta* with the name Honesty.

Overlooking the individual and the actual yields concepts, just as it yields forms, whereas nature knows neither forms nor concepts, hence no species, but only what remains for us an inaccessible and indefinable X. For even the distinction we draw between the individual and the species is anthropomorphic and does not stem from the essence of things, though neither can we say that it does not correspond to the essence of things, for that would be a dogmatic assertion and as such just as indemonstrable as its counterpart.

What, then, is truth? A mobile army of metaphors, metonymies, anthropomorphisms—in short, a sum of human relations that have been poetically and rhetorically intensified, translated, and embellished, and that after long use

strike a people as fixed, canonical, and binding: truths are illusions of which one has forgotten that they are illusions, metaphors that have become worn-out and deprived of their sensuous force, coins that have lost their imprint and are now no longer seen as coins but as metal. We still don't know where the drive to truth comes from, for we have hitherto heard only of the obligation to be truthful, which society imposes in order to exist—that is, the obligation to use the customary metaphors, hence, morally expressed, the obligation to lie in accordance with a fixed convention, to lie in droves in a style binding for all. Man forgets, of course, that this is how things are; he therefore lies in this way unconsciously and according to centuries-old habits—and precisely *by means of this unconsciousness*, precisely by means of this forgetting, he arrives at the feeling of truth. A moral impulse pertaining to truth is awoken out of this feeling of being obligated to desig-

nate one thing red, another cold, a third mute: in contrast to the liar, whom no one trusts, whom everyone shuns, man proves to himself how venerable, trustworthy, and useful truth is. As a *rational* being he now submits his actions to the rule of abstractions: no longer does he let himself be swept away by sudden impressions, by intuitions, he first generalizes all these impressions into paler, cooler concepts in order to hitch the wagon of his life and his action to them. Everything that distinguishes man from beast hinges on this capacity to dispel intuitive metaphors in a schema, hence to dissolve an image into a concept. For in the realm of those schemata something becomes possible that could never be achieved by intuitive first impressions, namely, the construction of a pyramidal order of castes and degrees, creating a new world of laws, privileges, subordinations, and boundary demarcations, which now stands over against the other intuitive

world of first impressions as the more fixed, more universal, more familiar, more human, hence something regulatory and imperative. Whereas every metaphor of intuition is individual and without equal and so always knows how to escape all classification, the great edifice of concepts exhibits the rigid regularity of a Roman columbarium* and in logic exhales the severity and coolness proper to mathematics. Whoever has felt that breath will scarcely believe that concepts, too, as bony and eight-cornered as dice, and just as moveable, are but the lingering *residues of metaphors*, and that the illusion of the artistic rendering of a nerve stimulus into images is, if not the mother, then at least the grandmother of every concept. In this dice game of concepts, however, "truth" means using every die as it is marked, counting

---

* A catacomb with separate niches housing urns that contained the ashes of the dead.

its dots precisely, establishing correct classifi-
cations, and never violating the order of castes
and rankings of class. Just as the Romans and
Etruscans carved up the sky with rigid mathematical lines, installing a god in each circum-
scribed space as in a *templum*, so, too, every
people has above it just such a mathematically
divided heaven of concepts and understands
the demand of truth to mean that each concept god is to be found only in *its own* sphere.
In this, one may well admire man as a great
architectural genius who manages to erect an
infinitely complicated cathedral of concepts
on shifting foundations and flowing water. Of
course, in order to rest on such foundations, it
must be a structure made as if of spiderwebs,
delicate enough to be carried away by the
waves, firm enough not to be blown apart by
the wind. Measured thus, man as architectural
genius far surpasses the bee: the latter builds
with wax, which it gathers from nature; man

builds with the much more delicate material of concepts, which he must first fabricate from out of himself. In this, he is to be admired—but not on account of his drive to truth, to the pure cognition of things. If someone hides a thing behind a bush, then looks for it and finds it again in the same place, the seeking and finding are not much to brag about; yet this is how matters stand with the seeking and finding of "truth" in the realm of reason. If I give a definition of "mammal" and then, after inspecting a camel, declare, "Behold, a mammal," a truth has indeed been brought to light, but one of limited value, by which I mean it is thoroughly anthropomorphic and contains not a single point that would be "true in itself," real and universally valid, apart from man. The seeker of such truths seeks at bottom only the metamorphosis of the world into man; he strives for an understanding of the world as a human thing and gains, in the best case, the feeling of

an assimilation. Like the astrologer who views the stars as in the service of human beings and as tied to their fortune and suffering, so, too, such a seeker views the entire world as bound to man, as the infinitely splintered echo of a primal sound, that of man, or as the reduplicated copy of a primal image, that of man. His procedure is to hold man up as the measure of all things, but in so doing he sets out from the error of believing that he has these things directly before him as pure objects. And so he forgets that the original metaphors of intuition were metaphors and takes them as the things themselves.

Only by forgetting that primitive world of metaphor, only by the hardening and stiffening of a mass of images that originally flowed forth hot and liquid from the primal power of human imagination, only by the unconquerable faith that *this* sun, *this* window, this table is a truth in itself—in short, only by man's for-

getting himself as subject, indeed as an *artistically creative* subject, does he live with some degree of peace, security, and consistency; if he could escape from the prison walls of that faith for just a moment, his "self-confidence" (*Selbstbewusstsein*) would be crushed instantly. It even requires some effort for him to admit to himself that an insect or a bird perceives a world utterly different from man's, and that it is senseless to ask which of the two perceptions of the world is correct, since that would have to be measured against a standard of *correct perception*, which is a nonexistent standard. Generally, however, correct perception—that is to say, the adequate expression of an object in a subject—strikes me as something contradictory and impossible; for between two such absolutely different spheres as subject and object there is no causality, no correctness, no expression, but at most an *aesthetic* comportment, by which I mean a suggestive rendering, a stam-

mering translation into an altogether foreign
language. Though even that would require a
freely poetic and freely inventive intermediate
sphere and mediating force. The word *appearance* contains many seductions, which is why I
avoid it as much as possible; for it is not true
that the essence of things appears in the empirical world. A painter with no hands who wants
to express the image hovering before him in
song will always reveal more with this transpo-
sition of spheres than the empirical world re-
veals of the essence of things. Even the relation
of a nerve stimulus to the image it produces
is in no way necessary. If, however, the very
same image is produced millions of times and
handed down through many generations and,
finally, in each case appears to all mankind as
the effect of the same cause, then ultimately
it acquires the same meaning for man, as if it
were the one necessary image, and as if that
relation of the original nerve stimulus to the

produced image were a strict causal relation; just as a dream, endlessly repeated, would be felt and judged to be thoroughly real. But the hardening and stiffening of a metaphor says nothing at all for the necessity and exclusive justification of that metaphor.

Anyone accustomed to such considerations has surely felt a deep suspicion of this kind of idealism whenever he has convinced himself of the eternal consistency, ubiquity, and infallibility of the laws of nature. Here, he concludes, as far as we can penetrate, from the heights of the telescopic to the depths of the microscopic, everything is certain, complete, infinite, lawlike, without gaps; science will be able to dig into these shafts forever with success, and all its findings will harmonize and not contradict one another. How little this resembles a product of imagination, for if it were that, it would have to betray the illusion and the unreality at some point. Against this, it must be said, first,

that if each of us had a different kind of sensory experience; if we ourselves could perceive now only as a bird, now as a worm, now as a plant; or if one of us saw the same stimulus as red, another as blue, and if a third even heard it as a sound, no one would talk about the supposed lawlike uniformity of nature but would instead conceive of it only as a highly subjective construct. Second, what is a law of nature for us, anyway? It is not known to us in itself but only in its effects, that is, in relation to other laws of nature, which are again known to us only as relations. All these relations in turn refer only to one another and are therefore thoroughly unintelligible to us in their essence; all we really know is what we bring to them—time, space, hence relations of succession and number. Everything wondrous that we marvel at in the laws of nature, that demands explanation and could lead us to a distrust of idealism, however, lies precisely and exclusively in the mathemati-

cal rigor and inviolability of the representations of time and space. This, though, we produce in ourselves and out of ourselves with the same necessity with which the spider spins its web; if we are constrained to conceive all things only under these forms, then it is no wonder that we do in fact conceive of all things in just these forms, for they all must bear in themselves the laws of number, and number is precisely what is most astonishing in things. The lawlike uniformity that so impresses us in the orbits of stars and in chemical processes ultimately coincides with those properties we ourselves bring to things, so that it is we who are impressing ourselves. From this, however, it follows that that artistic formation of metaphor, with which every sensation in us begins, already presupposes those forms and so finds completion in them; only the persistence of these primal forms explains the possibility of a structure of concepts subsequently being constituted from out of those

metaphors themselves. For this is nothing but an imitation of the relations of time, space, and number on the basis of metaphors.

2

As we have seen, it is *language*, in later ages *science*, that works originally at the construction of concepts. Just as the bee builds the cells and at the same time fills them with honey, so science works inexorably at that great columbarium of concepts, of burial sites of intuition, builds ever new and higher stories, props up, cleans, renews the old cells, and above all strives to fill that colossal, towering framework and fit the entire empirical word, that is, the anthropomorphic world, into it. And if the man of action binds his life to reason and its concepts in order not to be swept away and lose himself, the scientist builds his hut close to the tower of science in order

to assist it and find shelter for himself under the existing bulwark. And he needs shelter, for there are terrible forces constantly impinging upon him, holding out against scientific truth, "truths" of an entirely different kind, with the most diverse insignia.

That drive to the formation of metaphor, that fundamental drive of man that cannot be written off even for a moment, since one would thereby be writing off man himself, is in truth not overcome, indeed hardly even subdued, by the fact that it builds as a stronghold for itself out of its own fleeting products, namely, concepts, a regular and rigid world. It seeks out a new realm for its effects, another channel, and finds it in myth and in art generally.

It constantly confounds the rubrics and cells of concepts by arranging new figurations, metaphors, metonymies, constantly exhibiting the desire to make and remake the existing world of waking man as colorful, irregular, inconsequen-

tial, incoherent, charming, and eternally new
as the world of dreams. Indeed, waking man
himself is clear that he is awake thanks only to
the rigid and regular web of concepts and, for
that reason, occasionally comes to believe that
he is dreaming when that web of concepts is
torn apart momentarily by art. Pascal is right to
assert that if we had the same dream every night,
we would be as engaged by it as we are by the
things we see every day. "If an artisan were sure
of dreaming every night a full twelve hours that
he was king, I believe," says Pascal, "he would
be just as happy as a king who dreamed every
night for twelve hours that he was an artisan."*
Owing to what myth takes to be the constant
working of a miracle, the waking day of a mythi-
cally vibrant people, the ancient Greeks, for in-

---

* Blaise Pascal (1623–1662), French mathematician and philosopher. I have translated directly from Nietzsche's text. Pascal in fact says only "almost as happy." See Pascal, *Pensées*, A. J.
Krailsheimer, trans. (New York: Penguin, 1995), Series XXIX,
803 (386).

stance, is in fact more akin to dream than to the day of a sober scientific thinker. If every tree can on occasion speak as a nymph; if a god in the disguise of a bull can abduct virgins; if the goddess Athena herself is suddenly seen, accompanied by Pisistratus, driving a beautiful team of horses through the markets of Athens*—which is what every honest Athenian believed—then at every moment, just as in a dream, anything is possible, and all of nature swarms around man as if it were the masquerade of the gods, who amuse themselves by assuming different forms to deceive him.

Man himself, however, has an invincible tendency to let himself be deceived and is enchanted with happiness when the rhapsode tells him epic tales as if they were true, or when the actor in a play plays the king even more regally than he is in reality. The intellect, that master

---

* Herodotus, *Histories*, 1:60.

of dissimulation, is free and discharged from its other slavish duties, so long as it can deceive without *harming*, and then it celebrates its Saturnalia*; never is it more exuberant, richer, prouder, more agile, more daring. With creative delight it tosses metaphors together and displaces the boundary stones of abstraction, referring, for example, to a river as a moving pathway that carries man where he would otherwise walk. Now it has cast off all signs of servitude: it is usually at pains, with gloomy busyness, to show the way to some poor individual with a craving for existence, or, like a servant setting out in search of plunder and booty for his master, it has now become master and can wipe the expression of neediness from its face. Everything it does now, in contrast to its earlier deeds, involves dissimulation, just as

---

* Ancient Roman winter festival of eating, drinking, merriment, and the playful suspension or reversal of social roles, for example, those of masters and slaves.

what it did before involved distortion. It copies human life but sees it as a good thing and seems quite satisfied with it. Those enormous beams and planks of concepts to which man clings needily his whole life long to save himself are for the liberated intellect merely a scaffolding and plaything for its most daring feats; and in smashing it, mixing it up, reassembling it ironically, combining the most alien elements and separating those most closely connected, it demonstrates that it has no need of such makeshifts of neediness and will from now on be led not by concepts but by intuitions. There is no regular path leading from those intuitions into the land of ghostly schemata, of abstractions: there are no words for them; man falls silent when he sees them or speaks in strictly forbidden metaphors and egregious combinations of concepts in order to correspond creatively to the impression of the powerful present intuition, at least by demolishing and ridiculing the old conceptual restraints.

There are ages in which the rational man and the intuitive man stand side by side, the one fearful of intuition, the other scornful of abstraction; the latter as irrational as the former is inartistic. Both desire to rule over life: the former by knowing how to meet the most pressing needs with foresight, intelligence, and regularity, the latter, as an "over-joyous hero,"* by not seeing those needs and regarding life as real only when it feigns semblance and beauty. Where the intuitive man, as, for instance, in ancient Greece, brandishes his weapons more formidably and victoriously than his opponent, in favorable conditions a culture can emerge and art can establish dominion over life; all outward manifestations of that life are accompanied by that dissimulation, that denial of neediness, the radiance of metaphorical intuitions, and, above all,

---

* A description of Siegfried in Act III of Richard Wagner's opera *Twilight of the Gods*.

the immediacy of deceit. Neither such a man's house nor his way of walking nor his clothing nor his earthen jug look as if they were invented by need; everything in them seems to express a sublime happiness and an Olympian clear blue sky—and yet a playing at seriousness. Whereas the man led by concepts and abstractions uses them merely to ward off misfortune, deriving no happiness from the abstractions and seeking out the greatest possible freedom from misery, the intuitive man, standing in the midst of a culture, reaps from his intuitions not only a defense against evil but a continuous influx of illumination, cheerfulness, redemption. Of course, *when* he suffers, he suffers more intensely; he even suffers more often, since he doesn't know how to learn from experience and keeps falling into the same ditch he has fallen into before. He is then just as irrational in his sorrow as he is in his happiness; he cries out and has no consolation. How different things are for the Stoic

suffering the same misfortune, instructed by experience and ruling himself by means of concepts! Usually aspiring only to sincerity, truth, freedom from deception, and protection against beguiling attack, now, in misfortune, he delivers his masterpiece of dissimulation, just as the man of intuition did in happiness; his visage is not a wincing and expressive human face but like a mask with features of dignified symmetry; he doesn't cry out or even change his tone of voice. If a dark storm cloud bursts upon him, he wraps himself up in his cloak and slowly walks out from under it.

3

From *The Gay Science*
(1882)

5 4

Consciousness of appearance.—How wonderful and new and yet how eerie and ironic my knowledge makes me feel toward the whole of existence! I have *discovered* for myself that the old humanity and animality, indeed the entire primal age and past of all sentient beings, goes on composing, loving, hating,

inferring—I awoke suddenly in the midst of this dream, but only to the consciousness that I am still dreaming and that I *must* go on dreaming in order not to perish: just as the sleepwalker must go on dreaming to keep from falling down. What is "seeming" (*Schein*) to me now! Certainly not the opposite of some kind of being (*Wesen*)—what could I possibly say of any such being, other than the predicates of its seeming! Certainly not a dead mask that one could put on some unknown X, and indeed take off! For me, seeming is what is truly effective and alive, going so far in its self-mockery as to make me feel that here there is seeming and ghost lights and spirit dances, and nothing more—that among all those dreaming, I, too, the "knower," dance my dance; that one who knows is a means of drawing out the earthly dance and in this way belongs among the masters of ceremony of existence; and that the sublime consistency

and interconnectedness of all knowledge is and will be perhaps the highest means of *sustaining* the universality of dreaming and the understanding all these dreamers have among themselves, and so, too, even *the duration of the dream.*

110

Origin of knowledge.—Over vast stretches of time, the intellect produced nothing but errors; some of them turned out to be useful and species-preserving: whoever hit upon or inherited them waged the battle for themselves and their off-spring with better luck. Such erroneous articles of faith, which were further passed on and finally became almost the basic endowment of the human species, are, for example: that there are enduring things; that there are equal things; that there are things, materials, bodies; that a

thing is what it appears to be; that our will is free; that what is good for me is also good in and for itself. Only very late did the deniers and doubters of such propositions come on the scene—only very late did truth come on the scene as the weakest form of cognition. It seemed as if one could not live with it; our organism was geared to the opposite: all its higher functions, sense perception and every kind of sensation generally, worked with those fundamental errors, incorporated from archaic times. Moreover, even in the realm of knowledge those propositions became norms according to which one measured "true" and "untrue"—down to the most remote regions of pure logic. Thus, the *strength* of knowledge lies not in its degree of truth but in its age, its being incorporated, its character as a condition of life. Where life and knowledge seemed to come into conflict, there was never any serious contest; denial and doubt were considered madness. Those exceptional

thinkers, such as the Eleatics,* who, in spite of
everything, fixed and held fast to the opposites
of the natural errors, thought it possible also to
live this opposite: they invented the sage as the
man of immutability, impersonality, universality of intuition, as at once one and all, with a
special capacity for that inverted knowledge;
they were of the belief that their knowledge was
also the principle of *life*. But in order to assert
all this, they had to *deceive* themselves about
their own condition: they had to credit themselves with impersonality and duration without
change to misconceive the essence of knowledge, to deny the force of impulses in knowledge, and to conceive of reason in general as a
wholly free, self-originating activity; they closed
their eyes to the fact that they, too, had arrived

---

* Greek Presocratic philosophers from the ancient city of Elea,
a Greek colony in southern Italy. Parmenides, the founder of the
Eleatic school in the early fifth century B.C.E., used logical argument to deny the possibility of movement and change.

at their propositions in opposition to what was considered valid, or from a desire for tranquility, or disinterestedness, or domination. The more refined development of honesty and skepticism in the end rendered even these men impossible; their life and judgment, too, turned out to be parasitic on the age-old drives and fundamental errors of all sentient existence. That more refined honesty and skepticism arose where two antithetical propositions both seemed to *apply* to life, both being compatible with the fundamental errors, hence where it was possible to argue about greater and lesser degrees of *utility* for life; likewise, where new propositions showed themselves to be, if not especially useful to life, then at least not harmful either— expressions of an intellectual play impulse, innocent and happy like all play. Gradually the human brain filled itself with such judgments and convictions, and a ferment, a struggle, a craving for power emerged in this tangle. Not

only utility and delight but every kind of impulse took part in the fight over "truths": the intellectual fight became occupation, attraction, profession, duty, dignity; knowledge and striving for the true in the end took their place as a need among other needs. From then on, not only faith and conviction but also scrutiny, denial, mistrust, and contradiction became a *power*; all "evil" instincts were subordinated to knowledge, put in its service, and acquired the luster of the permissible, the honored, the useful, and finally the eye and the innocence of the *good*. Knowledge thus became part and parcel of life itself and as such an ever-increasing power—until finally knowledge and those age-old fundamental errors collided, both as life, both as power, both in the same man. The thinker: this is now the creature in whom the drive to truth and all those life-preserving errors wage their first battle, once the drive to truth has *proved* that it, too, is a life-preserving power.

Compared to the significance of this battle, all else is a matter of indifference: here, the ultimate question concerning the condition of life is posed, and here, the first attempt is made to answer the question with an experiment. To what extent can truth be incorporated?—that is the question, that is the experiment.

112

Cause and effect.—"Explanation" we call it, but "description" is what distinguishes us from earlier stages of knowledge and science. We describe better—we explain just as little as any of our predecessors. We have uncovered a manifold succession where the naive man and researcher of earlier cultures saw only two things, "cause" and "effect," as they put it; we have perfected the image of becoming, but we have neither gotten over the image nor gotten out of it. The

series of "causes" confronts us more completely in every case, and we infer: this and that must come first for that to come next—but we have thereby *grasped* nothing. In every chemical process, for example, quality appears to be a "miracle," just like all locomotion; no one has ever "explained" an impulse. How could we possibly explain! We work only with things that don't exist, with lines, planes, bodies, atoms, units of time, units of space—how is explanation even possible if we begin by making everything into an *image*, our image! It is enough to regard science as an attempt to humanize things as faithfully as possible; in describing things and their successions, we learn to describe ourselves ever more precisely. Cause and effect—there probably is no such a duality; in truth, a continuum stands before us, two segments of which we isolate, just as we perceive movement always only as isolated points and, so, do not really see but infer it. The abruptness with which many effects

leap out misleads us; it is an abruptness only for us. There is an endless abundance of events that elude us in this one second of abruptness. An intellect that saw cause and effect as a continuum and not, as we do, as arbitrary division and fragmentation, and which saw the flux of events—would reject the concept of cause and effect and deny all causal determination.

4

From *Beyond Good and Evil*
(1886)

PREFACE

Suppose truth is a woman—what then? Isn't it right to suspect that all philosophers, insofar as they were dogmatists, have had trouble understanding women? That the dreadful earnestness, the bumbling intrusiveness with which they have hitherto tried to approach truth were awkward and unbecoming ways of winning a woman over?

What is clear is that she has not let herself be won over—and today every kind of dogmatism stands there looking sad and discouraged. *If* it's still on its feet at all. For there are scoffers who insist that it has collapsed, that all dogmatism lies on the ground—moreover, that it's gasping for its final breath. Seriously though, there are good reasons to hope that all dogmatizing in philosophy, as solemnly, as definitively and proudly as it has conducted itself, may after all have been but a precious childishness and prelude, and perhaps it won't be long before we realize, time and again, *what* was once enough to serve as the cornerstone of the sublime and unconditioned philosophers' edifices those dogmatists used to build—some popular superstition from time immemorial (such as the soul superstition, which continues to cause mischief to this today as the superstition of the subject, of the I), perhaps a play on words, a seduction of grammar, or a bold generalization from so very narrow, so very personal, so very

human, all too human facts. The philosophy of
the dogmatist was, let us hope, no more than a
promise across millennia, like astrology was in
an earlier age, in whose service perhaps more
work, more money, more ingenuity and patience
has been lavished than hitherto for any real science—we have it and its "otherworldly" claims
to thank for the grand style of architecture in
Asia and Egypt. It seems that all great things, in
order to inscribe eternal demands in the heart
of man, must first walk the earth as monstrous
and frightening masks: dogmatic philosophy was
such a mask—for example, the Vedanta teaching
in Asia, Platonism in Europe. Let us not be ungrateful to it, though one must also admit that
the worst, the most protracted and most dangerous of all errors hitherto was a dogmatic error,
namely, Plato's invention of pure spirit and of the
Good in itself. Now that it has been overcome,
however, now that Europe breathes free of this in-
cubus and might at least enjoy a healthier—sleep,

we, *whose task is precisely to be awake*, are the heirs of all the strength fostered by the struggle against this error. Of course, it meant standing truth on its head and even denying *perspective*, the fundamental condition of all life, in speaking of spirit and the Good, as Plato did; indeed, like a physician, one might well ask, "How did such a disease manage to grow on the most beautiful plant of antiquity, on Plato? Did the evil Socrates corrupt him, after all? Could Socrates have been a corrupter of the youth, after all? And did he deserve the hemlock?— But the struggle against Plato or, to put it more intelligibly and for "the people," the struggle against Christian-ecclesiastical forces of millennia—for Christianity is Platonism for the "the people"—has created in Europe a magnificent tension of the spirit such as has never before existed on earth: with such a tightly strung bow, we can now shoot at the most distant targets. Of course, European man feels this tension as a kind of need and distress; and twice already attempts

have been made, in the grand style, to slacken the
bow: once by Jesuitism, then a second time by
democratic Enlightenment—which, with the aid
of freedom of the press and the reading of news-
papers, just might bring it about that the spirit no
longer feels itself in any kind of "need"! (The Ger-
mans invented gunpowder—all due respect there!
But, then, they made up for it: they invented the
printing press.) But we, we who are neither Jesu-
its nor democrats nor even sufficiently German,
we *good Europeans* and free, *very* free spirits—we
still have it, the full need of the spirit and the full
tension of the bow! And perhaps the arrow, too,
the task, who knows? The goal . . .

1

The will to truth, which still leads us on to many
a venture, that famous truthfulness of which all
philosophers hitherto have spoken with such

reverence—what questions has this will to truth put to us! What wondrous, wicked, questionable questions! That's already a long story—and yet it seems as if it's hardly begun. Is it any wonder that we finally become suspicious, lose patience, turn away impatiently? That *we ourselves* are also learning from this Sphinx how to pose questions? *Who* here is really asking us questions? *What* in us really wants "the truth"?— In fact, we paused for a long time before the question concerning the cause of this will—until, at last, we came to a complete standstill before an even more fundamental question. We asked about the *value* of this will. Granted, we want truth. *Why not rather* untruth? And uncertainty? Even ignorance?— The problem of the value of truth confronted us—or was it we who confronted it? Which of us here is Oedipus? Which the Sphinx? It's a rendezvous, it seems, of questions and question marks. And, incredible though it may seem, it strikes us that the problem has

never even been put—that we were the first ones to have seen it, to have our eye on it, to *venture* it. For it is a venture, and perhaps there is none greater.

4

The falsity of a judgment is not for us an objection to the judgment; this is perhaps where our new language will sound most foreign. The question is, To what extent is it life advancing, life preserving, species preserving, perhaps even species propagating? We are fundamentally inclined to assert that the falsest judgments (among them the synthetic judgments *a priori*) are for us the most indispensable, that without accepting the fictions of logic, without measuring reality against the wholly invented world of the unconditional, self-identical, without a constant falsification of the world through number,

man could not live—that to renounce false judgments would be to renounce life, to negate life.
To acknowledge untruth as a condition of life:
this surely means resisting customary value feelings in a dangerous way; and a philosophy that
ventures such a thing, just by doing so, places
itself beyond good and evil.

2 4

*O sancta simplicitas!** In what strange simplification and falsification man lives! One can
wonder endlessly, once one has accustomed
one's eyes to this wonder! How we have made
everything around us bright and free and easy
and simple! How we have managed to give our
senses carte blanche for everything superficial,
and our thinking a divine desire for brazen

---

* O holy simplicity!

leaps and bad inferences! How we have known
from the beginning how to protect our ignorance in order to enjoy a freedom we can barely
grasp—thoughtlessness, recklessness, hearti-
ness, cheerfulness in life! And only on this now
firm and granite foundation of ignorance could
science have arisen, the will to know founded
on a far more powerful will: the will not to
know, the will to the uncertain, to the untrue!
Not as its opposite, but—as its refinement!
Even if *language* cannot shed its awkward-
ness, here as elsewhere, and goes on speaking
of opposites where there are only degrees and
various shades of gradation; likewise, though
the ingrained tartuffery of morals, which now
belongs ineradicably to our "flesh and blood,"
twists the very words in our mouths, we knowers—here and there we grasp it and laugh at
how science at its best is best at wanting to
hold us fast in this *simplified*, altogether artifi-
cial, neatly constructed, neatly falsified world,

at how it so willingly-unwillingly loves error, because it, being alive—loves life!

2 5

After such a festive entrance, a serious word is in order: it is addressed to those who are most serious. Beware, you philosophers and friends of knowledge, and guard against martyrdom! Against suffering "for the sake of truth"! Even against defending yourselves! It spoils all the innocence and subtle neutrality of your conscience, it makes you headstrong against objections and red rags, it dumbs you down, makes you brutish and bullish, if, when battling danger, defamation, suspicion, expulsion, and even meaner consequences of animosity, you wind up having to play the role of protectors of truth on earth—as if "the truth" were some harmless and clumsy person in need of protectors! And you of all people, you Knights

of the Most Sorrowful Countenance,* my dear
loiterers and cobweb spinners of the spirit: in the
end, you know well enough that nothing hinges
on whether *you* are proved right, indeed that no
philosopher has ever been proved right, and that
there might be a more worthy truthfulness in
every little question mark you put behind your
favorite words and beloved doctrines (sometimes
even behind yourselves) than in all the solemn ges-
tures and trump cards played before accusers and
courts of law! No, step aside. Run to the shadows.
And have your masks and your finesse, that you
may not be recognized! Or that you may be feared
a little! And don't forget the garden, the garden
with golden trelliswork! And have people around
you who are like a garden—or like music on the
waters, in the evening, when the day has sunk into
memory— Choose that *good* solitude, free, playful, lighthearted solitude, which might even give

---

* An allusion to Miguel de Cervantes's *Don Quixote*.

you the right to be good, in some sense! How poi-
sonous, how cunning, how bad every protracted
war that cannot be waged with open force makes
us. How *personal* and protracted fear makes us,
a protracted spying on one's enemies, on poten-
tial enemies! These outcasts of society, those long
hunted, wickedly persecuted—the forced recluses,
the Spinozas or the Giordano Brunos—always in
the end become, albeit in the most spiritual guise,
and perhaps without knowing it themselves, sophisticated revenge seekers and poisoners (let
someone unearth the foundations of Spinoza's
ethics and theology!); not to mention the clum-
siness of moral indignation, which is a sure sign
that a philosopher has lost his philosophical sense
of humor. The martyrdom of the philosopher, his
"sacrifice to truth," brings to light the agitator and
the actor in him; and if one has hitherto regarded
him with mere artistic curiosity, in the case of
some philosophers it's not hard to understand the
dangerous wish to see them, too, in their degen-

eration (degenerating into "martyrs," crying out from their stages and rostrums). Except that with such a wish we must be clear about *what* we will get to see: just a satyr play, just an epilogue farce, just more proof that the actual long tragedy *has come to an end*—assuming that every philosophy arose as a long tragedy.

6 4

"Knowledge for its own sake"—this is the final snare set by morality: one thereby gets completely tangled up in it all over again.

6 5

The allure of knowledge would be meager, were it not that so much shame must be overcome along the way.

81

It is terrible to die of thirst in the ocean. Must you salt your truth so heavily that it no longer even—quenches thirst?

128

The more abstract the truth you want to teach, the more you must seduce the senses to it.

152

"Where the tree of knowledge stands, there is always paradise": thus speak the oldest and the youngest serpents.

177

Perhaps no one has yet been truthful enough about what "truthfulness" is.

230

Perhaps it's not entirely clear what I meant when I spoke of a "fundamental will of the spirit"—allow me to explain: That commanding something-or-other that people call "the spirit" wants to be master of itself and of its surroundings, and to feel itself to be master: it wills from multiplicity to simplicity, a binding, taming, domineering, and truly mastering will. Its needs and capacities are in this sense the same as those the physiologists attribute to everything that lives, grows, and multiplies. The strength of the

spirit to appropriate what is foreign manifests itself in a strong tendency to assimilate the new to the old, to simplify the manifold, to overlook or put aside what is utterly contradictory—just as it arbitrarily highlights certain features and lines in what is foreign, in every piece of the "external world," prescinding, falsifying just so. Its aim is thereby to incorporate new "experiences," to line things up in new rows—hence, growth or, more precisely, the *feeling* of growth, the feeling of increased strength. An apparently opposite drive of the spirit serves this same will, an abrupt opting for ignorance, willful exclusion, a closing of one's windows, an inner nay-saying to this or that thing, not letting things come near, a kind of defensive attitude against much that is knowable, a contentment with darkness, horizons closing in, a yea-saying and approving of ignorance: all this is necessary relative to its power to appropriate, its "digestive power," so to speak—and, really, "the spirit" is most like

a stomach. Here, too, belongs the occasional will of the spirit to let itself be deceived, perhaps with a capricious intimation that things are *not* such and such, that one merely accepts that such and such—a relishing of all uncertainty and ambiguity, a joyful self-delight in the arbitrary narrowness and secrecy of a nook, in the all too near, the foreground, the enlarged, the diminished, the shunted aside, the beautified, a self-delight in the willfulness of all these expressions of power. And here, too, belongs that by no means harmless willingness of the spirit to deceive other spirits and to dissemble before them, that constant stress and strain of a creative, formative, changeable force: the spirit enjoys the manyness and shiftiness of its masks, and it enjoys its feeling of security in them—it is indeed precisely its protean arts that defend and conceal it best!— *This* will to semblance, to simplification, to masks, to cloaks, in short, to surfaces—for every surface is a cloak—is

countered by that sublime inclination of the knower who takes things, and *wants* to take them, in a deep, manifold, and thorough way: as a kind of cruelty of intellectual conscience and taste, which every courageous thinker will recognize in himself, provided he has hardened and sharpened his eye for himself long enough and is accustomed to strict discipline and strict words. He will say, "There is something cruel in the inclination of my spirit"—let the virtuous and amiable try to talk him out of that! In fact, it would sound nicer if we were charged, rumored, praised for a kind of "wild honesty"—we free, *very* free spirits—and perhaps that will in fact be how it sounds, our—legacy? Meanwhile—for there is still time till then—we ourselves are least of all inclined to dress up with the same moral verbal tinsels and fringes: our entire work hitherto has made us sick of this style and its glaring opulence. These are beautiful, glittering, tinkling, festive words: honesty, love of truth, love

of wisdom, self-sacrifice for knowledge, heroism of the truthful man—there is something in them that makes one swell with pride. But we hermits and marmots, we convinced ourselves long ago in all the secrecy of a hermit's conscience that even this dignified pageantry of words belongs to the old false finery, junk, and gold dust of unconscious human vanity, and that the terrible underlying primary text *homo natura* must also be recognized beneath such flattering colors and painted surfaces. To translate man back into nature; to master the many vain and effusive interpretations and incidental meanings that have until now been scrawled and painted over that eternal primary text *homo natura*; to make sure that man stands henceforth before man, as he stands already today, hardened by the discipline of science, before the *rest* of nature, with unfrightened Oedipus eyes and sealed Odysseus ears, deaf to the lures of the old metaphysical bird catchers who have whistled to him all too

long, "You are more! You are higher! You are of a different origin!"—that may be a strange and insane task, but it is a *task*—who would deny it! Why would we choose it, this insane task? Or, put otherwise, "Why knowledge at all?" Everyone will ask us this. And we, pressed so hard, we who have already asked ourselves the same question a hundred times, we have found and find no better answer . . .

5

From *The Gay Science*, Book V
(1887)

344

How we, too, are still pious.—In science, convictions have no right of citizenship, so it is said and with good reason: only when they decide to descend to the modesty of a hypothesis, a provisional experimental standpoint, a regulative fiction, may they be granted admission and even a certain value in the realm of knowledge—though

always with the restriction of remaining under police surveillance, under police suspicion. But, considered more precisely, doesn't this mean: only when a conviction *ceases* to be a conviction may it gain admission to science? Wouldn't the cultivation of the scientific spirit begin with no longer allowing oneself to have any convictions? . . . Probably so; only it remains to ask whether *for this cultivation even to begin*, there must already be some conviction, indeed one so commanding and unconditional as to sacrifice all other convictions to itself. We see that even science rests on a faith; there is no such thing as "presuppositionless" science. The question whether *truth* is necessary must not only already have been answered affirmatively but must be affirmed to such a degree that the principle, the faith, the conviction is expressed: "There is *nothing more* necessary than truth, and compared to it everything else has only secondary value."— This unconditional will to truth: what

is it? Is it the will *not to let oneself be deceived*? Is it the will *not to deceive*? For the will truth could be interpreted in this second way, too—provided that one also subsumes under the generalization "I want not to deceive" the special case "I want not to deceive *myself.*" But why not deceive? And why not let oneself be deceived?— Note that the reasons for the former lie in an entirely different realm from those for the latter: one wants not to let oneself be deceived, on the assumption that it is harmful, dangerous, disastrous to be deceived—in this sense, science would amount to a far-sighted intelligence, a cautiousness, a utility, to which one could, however, fairly object: But why? Is not wanting to let oneself be deceived really less harmful, less dangerous, less disastrous? What do you know in advance of the character of existence to be able to decide whether the greater advantage is on the side of the unconditionally distrustful or the unconditionally trusting? But if both should be neces-

sary, great trust *and* great distrust, then whence does science derive its unconditional faith, the conviction on which it rests, that truth is more important than anything else, including every other conviction? Even this conviction could not have arisen if truth *and* untruth had both constantly shown themselves to be useful—which is the case. Hence, faith in science, which after all undeniably exists, cannot have had its origin in such a utility calculus but rather *in spite of* the fact that the uselessness and dangerousness of the "will to truth," of "truth at all costs," is constantly demonstrated to it. "At all costs": oh, we understand that well enough, once we have offered up and slaughtered one faith after another on this altar! Consequently, "will to truth" does *not* mean "I want not to let myself be deceived" but—there is no alternative—"I want not to deceive, not even myself": *and with that we stand on moral ground.* For you need only ask yourself, really ask, "Why do you not want to deceive?"

especially if it should seem—as it does seem!—
that life aims at semblance, I mean error, cheating, dissembling, delusion, self-delusion, and
when in fact the grand pageant of life has always
shown itself to be on the side of the most care-
free πολύτροποι.* Such a resolution, charitably
interpreted, might be a mere quixotism, a minor
mad folly; but it could also be something worse,
namely, a destructive principle hostile to life . . .
"Will to truth"—that could be a concealed will
to death. Thus, the question "Why science?"
leads back to the moral problem: *wherefore morality at all*, if life, nature, history are "amoral"?
No doubt, anyone who is truthful in that bold
and ultimate sense presupposed by faith in science *thereby affirms a world other* than that of
life, nature, and history; and insofar as he affirms this "other world," must he not precisely

---

* "Shifty, versatile, wily things": Homer uses the singular to describe Odysseus in the first line of the *Odyssey*.

thereby deny its counterpart, this world, *our* world? . . . You will of course have grasped what I'm getting at: namely, that it is still a *metaphysical faith* on which our faith in science rests—that even we knowing ones of today, we godless ones and antimetaphysicians, still also take *our* fire from the flame ignited by a faith thousands of years old, that Christian faith that was also Plato's faith, that God is truth, that truth is divine . . . But what if just this were to become ever more unbelievable, if nothing else were ever to prove itself divine, only error, blindness, lie—if God himself proved to be our longest lie?

3 5 4

On the "genius of the species."—[. . .] My idea, as you can see, is that consciousness does not really belong to the individual existence of man but to his community or herd nature; that, conse-

quently, it is finely developed only in relation to community and herd utility; and, consequently, that each of us, with the best will to *understand* ourselves as individually as possible, "to know ourselves," will always only bring to consciousness precisely what is nonindividual in ourselves, what is "average": that our thoughts themselves are constantly *overruled* by the character of consciousness—by the "genius of the species" dominating them—and translated back into the herd perspective. All our actions are at bottom incomparably personal, unique, endlessly individual, there is no doubt; but as soon as we translate them into consciousness, *they no longer seem so* . . . This is genuine phenomenalism and perspectivism, as *I* understand it: the nature of *animal consciousness* is such that the world we can be conscious of is only a world of surfaces and signs, a world generalized, made common— that everything that becomes conscious thereby *becomes* flat, thin, relatively stupid, general, a

sign, a herd signal; that all coming to conscious involves a vast and thoroughgoing corruption, falsification, superficialization, and generalization. Heightened consciousness is ultimately a danger, and whoever lives among the most conscious Europeans knows moreover that it's a sickness. As you might guess, it is not the opposition of subject and object that concerns me here—I leave that distinction to the epistemologists who have gotten caught in the snares of grammar (and folk metaphysics). It is even less the opposition of "thing in itself" and appearance, for we do not "know" nearly enough even to be entitled to *draw* such a distinction. We simply have no organ for *knowing*, for "truth": we "know" (or believe, or imagine) just as much as may be *useful* in the interests of the human herd, the species; and even what is here called "utility" is in the end only a faith, something imagined, and perhaps precisely the most disastrous stupidity that will one day do us in.

374

Our new "infinite."—How far the perspectival character of existence extends, or even whether it has any other character; whether an existence without interpretation, without "sense," does not become "nonsense"; whether, on the other hand, all existence is not essentially an *interpreting* existence—that cannot be decided, even by the most industrious and scrupulously conscientious analysis and self-examination of the intellect: for in that very analysis the human intellect cannot avoid seeing itself under its perspectival forms, and *only* in them. We cannot see around our own corner—it is a hopeless curiosity to want to know what other kinds of intellects and perspectives there *could* be: for example, whether some creature can experience time backward, or alternately forward and backward (which would be given along with another direction of life and another concept of cause and effect). But

today, I think, we are at least beyond the laughable immodesty of decreeing from our corner that one is *allowed* perspectives only from our corner. The world has instead become "infinite" for us once again inasmuch as we cannot deny the possibility that it *includes in itself infinite interpretations.* Once again the great shiver goes down our spine—but who would want to go on to deify *this* monstrosity of an unknown world in the same old way? And henceforth worship the unknown as "The Unknown"? Oh, there are too many *ungodly* possibilities of interpretation bound up with this unknown, too much devilry, stupidity, foolishness of interpretation—our own human, even all too human foolishness, which we know . . .

6

From *On the Genealogy of Morals*, Third Essay

(1887)

11

[. . .] an ascetic life is a self-contradiction: a *ressentiment* rules here without equal, that of an insatiable instinct and will to power, wanting to be master not of something in life but of life itself, of its deepest, strongest, most primal conditions; here, an attempt is made to use force to stop up the wellsprings of force; here, physi-

ological thriving itself is viewed with envy and derision, especially its expression, beauty, joy; while pleasure is sensed and *sought* in deformity, atrophy, pain, accident, the ugly, the self-inflicted wound, self-denial, self-flagellation, self-sacrifice. This is all paradoxical in the highest degree: here, we stand before a discord that *wants* to be discordant, that *enjoys* itself in this suffering and becomes ever more self-confident and triumphant to the extent that its own presupposition, its own physiological capacity for life, *diminishes*. "Triumph in the final agony itself": the ascetic ideal has hitherto fought under this superlative banner; in this riddle of seduction, in this image of delight and torment it recognizes its brightest light, its salvation, its final victory. *Crux, nux, lux**—in it, these three are one.

---

* Cross, nut, light.

1 2

Suppose that such an embodied will to contradiction and counternature is brought to
philosophize—on what will it unleash its inner
willfulness? On whatever it experiences most
certainly as true, as real: it will seek *error* precisely where the real vital instinct finds truth
most unconditionally. It will, for example,
like the ascetics of Vedanta philosophy, dis-
parage bodily being as illusion, likewise pain,
plurality, the entire conceptual opposition of
"subject" and "object"—errors, nothing but
errors! Renouncing belief in its I, denying its
own "reality": what a triumph!—and not just
over the senses, over appearances, but a far
greater kind of triumph, a violation and a cruelty to *reason*: this lustfulness reaches its peak
when the ascetic self-contempt, self-ridicule
of reason decrees, "There *is* a realm of truth
and being, but reason is *barred* from it!" . . .

(Incidentally, even in the Kantian concept of the "intelligible character of things" there is still a remnant of this lascivious ascetic discord that loves to turn reason against reason: "intelligible character" in Kant means a kind of constitution of things of which the intellect comprehends just this much, that it is for the intellect—*utterly incomprehensible*.) Finally, let us not be ungrateful, we knowers, for such resolute reversals of customary perspectives and valuations with which the spirit has so wickedly and so uselessly ravaged itself for so long: to see differently like this for once, to *want* to see differently, is no small cultivation and preparation of the intellect for its eventual "objectivity"—the latter understood not as "disinterested contemplation" (which is incoherent and nonsense) but as the ability to hinge and unhinge and *to hold sway over* its pro and con, so that one knows how to make the very *diversity* of perspectives and affective

interpretations useful for knowledge. Henceforth, my dear philosophers, let us guard against the dangerous old conceptual fiction that posited a "pure, will-less, painless, timeless subject of knowledge"; let us guard against the snares of such contradictory concepts as "pure reason," "absolute spirit," "knowledge in itself": for this always demands thinking of an eye that cannot possibly be thought, an eye that would have no direction at all, in which the active and interpretive forces— through which, after all, seeing first becomes seeing something—are to be disabled, are to be lacking; here, what is demanded of the eye is always something nonsensical and incoherent. There is *only* perspectival seeing, *only* perspectival "knowing"; and *the more* affects we bring to expression about any one thing, *the more* eyes—different eyes—we know how to bring to bear on the same thing, the more complete will be our "concept" of that thing,

our "objectivity." To eliminate will altogether, though, to suspend the affects, one and all, supposing we could do it—what, wouldn't that mean *castrating* the intellect? . . .

24

—And now look, by way of contrast, at those rarer cases I mentioned, the last idealists today among philosophers and scholars: do we find in them perhaps the sought-after *opponents* of the ascetic ideal, its *counter-idealists*? To be sure, they *believe* themselves such, these "unbe-lievers" (for that's what they are, all of them); it seems that being opponents of this ideal is precisely their last article of faith, so earnest are they on this point, so passionate are their words, their deeds—need it therefore be *true* what they believe? . . . We "knowers" are by now mistrustful of all kinds of believers; our

mistrust has gradually accustomed us to infer the very opposite of what was once inferred: namely, wherever the strength of a belief comes very much to the fore, we infer a certain weakness of demonstration, an *improbability* of that which is believed. We do not deny that faith "beatifies": *for that very reason* we deny that faith *proves* anything—a strong faith that beatifies raises suspicion against what it believes; what it proves is not "truth" but a certain probability—of *deception*. How do things stand in this case?— These modern-day nay-sayers and standoffish ones, those who are unconditional on a single point—the claim to intellectual cleanliness—these hard, strict, abstinent, heroic spirits who constitute the honor of our age, all these pale atheists, anti-Christians, immoralists, nihilists, these skeptics, ephetics, *hectics* of the spirit (for this they are, one and all, in some sense), these last idealists of knowledge in whom alone intellectual

conscience today dwells and is embodied—they
in fact believe themselves to be as free as possible of the ascetic ideal, these "free, *very* free
spirits": and yet, to intimate to them what they
themselves cannot see—for they're standing too
close to themselves—this ideal is precisely *their*
ideal, too; they themselves represent it, and perhaps no one else; they themselves are its most
spiritualized product, its most advanced war-
riors and scouts, its most captious, most delicate, most elusive form of seduction— If I am
any kind of guesser of riddles, let me try with
this proposition! . . . They are far from being *free*
spirits: *for they still believe in truth* . . . When
the Christian crusaders in the Orient came
across that invincible order of Assassins, that
order of free spirits par excellence whose lower
ranks lived in an obedience such as no order
of monks has ever attained, they also acquired
somehow or other a hint of that symbol and
watchword reserved only for the highest ranks,

as their *secretum*: "Nothing is true, everything is permitted." . . . Now *that* was *freedom* of the spirit, *with that*, faith in truth itself was *renounced* . . . Has any European, any Christian free spirit ever strayed into this proposition and its labyrinthine *consequences*? Does he know the Minotaur of this cave *from experience*? . . . I doubt it; in fact, I know it's not so: nothing is more foreign to those who are unconditional on a single point, these *so-called* "free spirits," than freedom and unfettering in this sense; in no respect are they more firmly bound; it is precisely in their faith in truth that they are, like no one else, firm and unconditional. I know all this from too close up, perhaps: that admirable abstemiousness of philosophers to which such faith obliges one; that stoicism of the intellect that in the end forbids the No just as strictly as it does the Yes; that *wanting* to stand still before the factual, the *factum brutum*; that fatalism of the "*petits faits*" (*ce petit faitalisme*, as I call it), in

which French science now seeks a kind of moral superiority over German science; that general *renunciation* of interpretation (of forcing, setting straight, abridging, omitting, padding, inventing, falsifying, and whatever else belongs to the *essence* of all interpreting)—this, broadly speaking, expresses as much asceticism of virtue as any abnegation of sensibility (it is, at bottom, simply a mode of that abnegation). But what it *forces* you into, that unconditional will to truth, is *faith in the ascetic ideal itself,* even if as its unconscious imperative—make no mistake about it—this is faith in a *metaphysical* value, the value *in itself of truth*, as sanctioned and guaranteed in that ideal alone (it stands or falls with that ideal). There is, strictly speaking, no such thing as "presuppositionless" science—the very idea is unthinkable, paralogical: a philosophy, a "faith" must always be there first, so that from it science can acquire a direction, a sense, a limit, a method, a *right* to exist. (Anyone who under-

stands this the other way around, who sets out, for example, to put philosophy "on a rigorous scientific foundation," first has to stand not only philosophy but truth itself *on its head*—the grossest violation of decency there can be in the presence of two such dignified ladies!) Yes, there is no doubt—and here I refer to my *Gay Science*, Book V (§344)—"anyone who is truthful in that bold and ultimate sense presupposed by faith in science *thereby affirms a world other* than that of life, nature, and history; and insofar as he affirms this 'other world,' must he not precisely thereby deny its counterpart, this world, *our* world? . . . It is still a *metaphysical faith* on which our faith in science rests—even we knowing ones of today, we godless ones and antimetaphysicians, still also take *our* fire from the flame ignited by a faith thousands of years old, that Christian faith that was also Plato's faith, that God is truth, that truth is divine . . . But what if just this were to become ever more

unbelievable, if nothing else were ever to prove itself divine, only error, blindness, lie—if God himself proved to be our *longest lie*?"— Here we must pause and reflect a while. Science henceforth stands *in need of* justification (which is not to say that it has one). On this question, just look at the most ancient and the most recent philosophies: in none of them is there any awareness of the extent to which the will to truth itself stands in need of justification; there is a gap here in every philosophy—why is that? Because the ascetic ideal has hitherto *dominated* all of philosophy; because truth was posited as being, as God, as the highest authority; because truth was simply not *allowed* to be a problem. Do we understand this "allowed"?— From the moment faith in the god of the ascetic ideal is repudiated, *there is a new problem as well*: that of the *value* of truth. The will to truth stands in need of critique—here we define our own task— the value of truth must be experimentally *called*

into question . . . (Anyone who finds this stated too abruptly is advised to read the section of *The Gay Science* bearing the title "How we, too, are still pious" (§344), or better yet the entire Book V of that work, as well as the preface to *Daybreak*.)

7

From *The Will to Power*
(1883–1888)

4 8 7

Must not all philosophy in the end bring to light the presuppositions upon which the movement of *reason* rests: our *belief in the "I"* as a substance, as the sole reality according to which we attribute reality to things generally? The oldest "realism" finally comes to light—at the same time as the entire religious history of mankind is rec-

ognized as the history of the soul superstition. *There is a limit here:* our thinking itself involves that belief (with its distinction between substance and accident, deed and doer, etc.); letting go of it means no longer being allowed to think.

That a belief, however necessary it may be for the preservation of a creature, has nothing to do with truth, one can see, for example, in the fact that we have to believe in time, space, and motion, but without feeling constrained to grant them absolute reality.

4 8 8

Psychological derivation of our belief in reason.— The concept of "reality," "being," is drawn from our "subject"-feeling.

"Subject": interpreted from out of ourselves, so that the "I" counts as substance, as the cause of all doings, as doer.

The logico-metaphysical postulates—the belief in substance, accident, attribute, etc.—gets its force of conviction from our being accustomed to regard all our actions as following from our will: so that the I, as substance, does not vanish in the manifold of change.—*But there is no will.*

We have no categories at all allowing us to distinguish a "world in itself" from a "world as appearance." All our *categories of reason* are of sensuous origin, read off of the empirical world. "The soul," "the I"—the history of our concepts shows that here, too, the oldest distinction ("breath," "life") . . .

If there is nothing material, neither is there anything immaterial. The concept no longer *contains* anything.

No subject-"atom": the sphere of a subject constantly *increasing* or *decreasing*, the midpoint of a system constantly *adjusting* itself; in the case where it cannot organize the mass it has acquired, it breaks in two. On the other hand, it can refash-

ion a weaker subject into its functionary without destroying it and, to a certain degree, form a new unity with it. No "substance," but rather something that in itself strives for enhancement; and which only indirectly wants to "preserve" itself (it wants to *surpass* itself—).

493

Truth is the kind of error without which a particular kind of living creature could not live. The value for *life* is ultimately decisive.

494

It is improbable that our "knowledge" should reach farther than it must extend for the preservation of life. Morphology shows us how the senses and the nerves, as well as the brain, de-

velop in proportion to the difficulty of finding nourishment.

4 9 5

If the morality of "thou shalt not lie" is rejected, "the sense for truth" must legitimate itself before a different tribunal: as a means of the preservation of man, *as will to power.*

The same goes for our love of the beautiful: it, too, is a *will to shape.* The two senses stand side by side; the sense for the real is a means of acquiring the power to shape things as one pleases. The delight in shaping and reshaping—a primal delight! We can *comprehend* only a world we ourselves have made.

4 9 6

On the *multifariousness* of knowledge.—To trace

one's relation to many other things (or to a kind—how can that be "knowledge" of something *other*!) This kind of knowing and recognizing is itself already among the conditions of existence—so that the conclusion that there could be no kind of intellect (even for us) other than the one that preserves us, is too hasty: this de facto condition of existence is perhaps only accidental, perhaps in no way necessary.

Our cognitive apparatus is not *designed* for "knowledge."

497

The most firmly believed *a priori* "truths" are, for me—*provisional assumptions*, e.g., the law of causality, very well rehearsed habits of believing, so deeply incorporated that *not* believing them would drive the race to extinction. But are they for that reason truths? What a conclusion!

As if the truth could be proved by man's con-
tinuing to exist!

5 0 3

The entire cognitive apparatus is an apparatus for
abstraction and simplification—designed not for
knowledge but for *gaining control* of things: "end"
and "means" are as far from what is essential as
are "concepts." With "end" and "means" one
gains control of the process (one *invents* a process
that can be grasped); "concepts," however, being
the "things" that make up the process.

5 0 6

First *images*—to explain how images arise in the
mind. Then *words*, applied to images. Finally
concepts, possible only when there are words—

a subsuming of many images under something not intuitive but audible (a word). The small bit of emotion that arises with the "word," hence with the intuition of similar images for which there is a single word—this weak emotion is the common element, the basis of the concept. The basic fact is that weak sensations are regarded as equal, sensed *as the same*. Hence the confusion of two closely contiguous sensations in the *ascertaining* of those sensations—but who is doing the ascertaining? *Believing* is the primal beginning even in every sense impression; a kind of yea-saying the *first* intellectual activity! A "holding-true" in the beginning! Thus to explain how a "holding-true" arose! What sort of sensation lies *behind* "true"?

507

The *valuation* "I believe that such and such is so" as the *essence* of "*truth*." *Conditions of pres-*

ervation and *growth* are expressed in valuations. All our *cognitive organs and senses* are developed only with regard to conditions of preservation and growth. Trust in reason and its categories, in dialectic, hence the *valuation* of logic, proves only their *usefulness* for life, proved by experience—*not* their "truth."

That an abundance of *belief* must be present; that *judgments* may be made; that doubt with regard to all essential values be *lacking*—that is the presupposition of every living thing and its life. Hence that something must be held to be true, *not* that something *is* true.

"The *true* and the *apparent* world"—I have traced this antithesis back to *relations of values*. We have projected *our* conditions of preservation as *predicates of being* generally. We must be firm in our beliefs in order to thrive; consequently, we have made the "true" world one not of change and becoming but of *being*.

5 1 2

Logic is bound to the condition: *assume there are identical cases*. In fact, for logical thought and inference to operate, this condition must be treated as if having been fulfilled. That is, the will to logical truth can be exercised only after a fundamental *falsification* of all events has been assumed. From which it follows that a drive is at work here that has two means at its disposal: first falsification, then implementation of its own point of view—logic does *not* stem from the will to truth.

5 1 5

Not to "know" but to schematize—to impose on chaos as much regularity and form as is required by our practical needs.

In the formation of reason, logic, the categories, *need* is what has been decisive: the need not

to "know" but to subsume, to schematize, for the purpose of understanding, of calculation— (Adjustment, devising ways of assimilating, of equating—the same process that every sense impression undergoes—such is the development of reason!) Here, no preexisting "idea" is at work; rather, the practicality that only if we see things crudely and leveled off do they become calculable and manageable for us— *Finality* in reason is an effect, not a cause: with any other kind of reason, to which there are constant impulses, life miscarries—it becomes unsurveyable—too unequal—

The categories are "truths" only in the sense that they are life conditioning for us: Euclidean space is one such conditioning "truth." (To speak plainly: since no one will maintain that it was necessary that man should even exist, reason, as well as Euclidean space, is a mere idiosyncrasy of a particular species of animal, and just one among many others . . .)

The subjective constraint of not being able to contradict here is a biological constraint: the instinct of utility of inferring as we infer is rooted in our bodies, we virtually *are* this instinct . . . But what naiveté to derive from this an argument that we are in possession of a "truth in itself"! . . . Not being able to contradict demonstrates an incapacity, not a "truth."

530

Theological prejudice in Kant, his unconscious dogmatism, his moralistic perspective, was dominant, guiding, commanding.

The πρῶτον ψεῦδος*: how is the fact of *knowledge* possible? What is knowledge? If we do not *know* what knowledge is, we cannot possibly answer the question whether there is or can

---

* False premise, original error.

be knowledge; I cannot even rationally pose the question "What is knowledge?" Kant *believes* in the fact of knowledge; what he wants is a bit of naiveté: *knowledge of knowledge!*

"Knowledge is judgment!" But judgment is a *belief* that something is such and such! And *not* knowledge! "All knowledge consists in synthetic judgments" with the character of *universal validity* (the matter stands thus and not otherwise in all cases), with the character of *necessity* (the opposite of the assertion can never occur).

The *legitimacy* of the belief in knowledge is always presupposed, just as the legitimacy of the feeling of a judgment of conscience is presupposed. Here, *moral ontology* is the *ruling* prejudice.

The conclusion is therefore: (1) there are assertions that we take to be universally valid and necessary; (2) the character of necessity and universal validity cannot stem from experience; (3) consequently, it must be *grounded in something*

else and have another cognitive source, outside of experience!

(Kant concludes that (1) there are assertions that are valid only under a certain condition; (2) this condition is that they stem not from experience but from pure reason.)

Thus, the question is: What is the ground of our *belief* in the truth of such assertions? No, what causes it? But the *source of a belief*, of a strong conviction, is a psychological problem; and it is often a very limited and narrow experience that brings about such a belief! It *already presupposes* that there are not only "data *a posteriori*" but also "data *a priori*"—"prior to experience." Necessity and universal validity can never be given by experience: so, why should we think that they are present without experience at all?

There are no individual judgments!

An individual judgment is never "true," never knowledge; only in *connection*, in *relation* to many judgments is there any guarantee.

What distinguishes true from false beliefs? What is knowledge? He "knows" it, that is heavenly!

Necessity and universal validity can never be given by experience! Hence independently of experience, prior to all experience! Any insight that occurs *a priori*, hence independently of all experience, is *from mere reason*, "a *pure* form of knowledge"!

"The principles of logic, the principle of identity and the law of noncontradiction, are pure forms of knowledge, since they precede all experience."— They are not forms of knowledge, however, but *regulative articles of faith*!

To establish the apriority (the pure rationality) of mathematical judgments, space *must be grasped as a form of pure reason*.

Hume declared, "There are no synthetic *a priori* judgments."* Kant says, But there are!

---

* David Hume (1711–1776), Scottish philosopher and historian.

Those of mathematics! And so, if there are such judgments, there is perhaps also metaphysics, a knowledge of things by means of pure reason!

Mathematics is possible under conditions under which metaphysics is *never* possible. All human knowledge is either experience or mathematics.

A judgment is synthetic: i.e., it combines different representations.

It is *a priori*: i.e., the combination is a universally valid and necessary one, which can never be given by sense experience but only by pure reason.

If there are to be synthetic *a priori* judgments, then reason must be capable of combining: combining is a form. Reason must exhibit a form-giving capacity.

Although it fairly captures Hume's view, the quotation is a fiction. The terminology is Kant's, not Hume's.

5 3 1

Judging is our oldest faith, our most accustomed holding-true or -untrue, asserting or denying, a certainty that something is so and not otherwise, a faith that here we have really "known"—what is believed to be true in all judgments?

What are *predicates*? We have viewed change in us not as change in us but as something "in itself," something foreign to us, something we only "perceive"; and we have posited it *not* as a happening but as a being, as a "property"—and have moreover invented an entity to which it adheres, i.e., we have regarded the *effect* as *effective* and the *effecting* as a *being*. Even in this formulation, however, the concept "effect" is still arbitrary: for from those changes that occur in us and of which we firmly believe ourselves *not* to be the cause, we infer only that they must be effects, according to the inference "For every change there is an instigator"—but this conclu-

sion is already mythology: it *separates* what is effective from the effecting. If I say, "the lightning flashes," I have posited the flashing once as activity and then again as subject and thus added to the event a being, which is not identical with the event but rather *remains*, is, and does not "become."— *To regard the event as an effecting,* and the effect as being: that is the *double* error, or interpretation, of which we are guilty.

532

Judgment—the belief that "this and that is so." Thus, judgment contains the avowal that an "identical case" has been encountered: it thus presupposes comparison, with the aid of recollection. Judgment does not create the appearance of an identical case. Rather, it believes it perceives one; it works under the presupposition that there are in general identical cases. What

is that function, which must be much older, operative much earlier, which levels off and as- similates? What is that second one, which on the basis of the first, etc. "That which excites the same sensations is the same"; but what is the "That" that makes sensations the same, "takes" them to be the same?— There could be no judgments at all if a kind of equalization had not first been exercised within the sensations: recollection is only possible with a constant un- derscoring of what is already accustomed, expe- rienced.— Before anything is judged, the process of assimilation must already be completed: thus, here, too, there is an intellectual activity that does not enter into consciousness, like pain fol- lowing from an injury. An inner event probably corresponds to all organic functions, hence an assimilating, eliminating, growing, etc.

Essential: to begin with the *body* and use it as a guiding thread. It is the much richer phe- nomenon and affords clearer observation. Belief

in the body is better established than belief in the mind.

"However strongly something may be believed, that is no criterion of truth." But what is truth? Perhaps a kind of belief that has become a condition of life? Then, of course, strength would be a criterion, e.g., with regard to causality.

5 3 3

Logical certainty, transparency, as criterion of truth (*"omne illud verum est, quod clare et distincte percipitur,"** Descartes): the mechanical hypothesis concerning the world is thereby desirable and credible.

But that is a crude confusion: like *simplex sigillum veri.†* How do we know that the true

---

* Whatever is clearly and distinctly perceived is true.
† Simplicity is the sign of truth.

constitution of things stands in this relation to our intellect?— Couldn't it be otherwise? That the hypothesis that gives the intellect the greatest feeling of power and security is the most *preferred*, *valued*, and *consequently* characterized as *true*?— The intellect posits its freest and strongest capacity and ability as the criterion of the most valuable, consequently of the *true* . . .

"True":

- from the side of feeling—what arouses feeling most forcefully ("I");
- from the side of thinking—what gives thinking the greatest feeling of strength;
- from the side of touching, seeing, hearing—that which calls for the greatest resistance.

Thus, it is the highest degree of activity that awakens belief in the "truth," that is, the *reality*, of the object. The feeling of strength, of

struggle, of resistance convinces us that there *is* something here being resisted.

5 3 4

The criterion of truth lies in the intensification of the feeling of power.

5 3 5

"Truth": in my way of thinking this designates not necessarily the opposite of error but in the most fundamental cases only the position of various errors in relation to one another. Perhaps one is older or deeper than another, maybe even ineradicable, inasmuch as an organic being of our kind could not live without it; while other errors do not tyrannize us in the same way as conditions of life but, when measured against

such "tyrants," can instead be set aside and "re-futed."

An assumption that is irrefutable—why should it for that reason be "true"? This proposition will perhaps outrage logicians, who regard *their* limits as the limits of *things*—but I long ago declared war on this logicians' optimism.

5 3 6

Everything simple is merely imaginary, not "true." But what is real, what is true, is neither one nor even reducible to one.

5 3 7

What is truth?—Inertia; the hypothesis that produces satisfaction; the least expenditure of mental strength, etc.

5 3 8

First proposition. The *easier* mode of thought triumphs over the harder; as dogma: *simplex sigillum veri.—Dico**: the idea that *clarity* demonstrates something about truth is perfectly childish—

Second proposition. The doctrine of *being*, of thing, of hard and fast unities, is *a hundred times easier* than the doctrine of *becoming*, of development—

Third proposition. Logic was intended as *facilitation*: as a *means of expression*—not as truth . . . Later it came to function as *truth*—

5 3 9

Parmenides said, "One cannot think what is

_____

* I say.

not"; we are at the other end and say, "Whatever can be thought must surely be a fiction."

540

There are many kinds of eyes. Even the Sphinx has eyes—and consequently there are many kinds of "truths," and consequently there is no truth.

586

The "True" and the "Apparent World"

A

The *seductions* that emanate from this concept are of three kinds:

a. An *unknown* world: we are inquisitive adventurers—the known world seems to

make us weary (the danger of the concept lies in its insinuating that "this"
world is known to us . . .).

b. *Another* world, where things are different:
something in us recalculates; our silent
acquiescence, our reticence thereby lose
their value—perhaps everything will be
fine, we haven't hoped in vain . . . The
world where things are different, where we
ourselves (who knows?) are different . . .

c. A *true* world: this is the most amazing
trick and offense that has ever been per-
petrated against us; so much has gotten
encrusted on the word *true* that we un-
wittingly offer it all up as a present to
the "true world"—the *true* world must
also be a *truthful* world, one that doesn't
cheat us, doesn't make fools of us: believing in it is virtually having to believe (out
of decency, as it is among those worthy
of confidence).

- The concept "the *unknown* world" insinuates that *this* world is "known" (as tedious);
- the concept "the *other* world" insinuates that the world could be otherwise—supersedes necessity and fate (unnecessary to *submit*, to *adapt*);
- the concept "the true world" insinuates that this world is untruthful, deceitful, dishonest, inauthentic, inessential—and, consequently, not a world adapted to our needs (inadvisable to adapt to it; better to resist it).

We therefore *divest* from "this" world in three ways:

a. With our *inquisitiveness*—as if the most interesting part were elsewhere;

b. With our *submission*—as if it were not necessary to submit; as if this world were not a necessity of the highest order;

   c.   With our *sympathy* and respect—as if this world did not deserve them, were impure, had been dishonest with us . . .

In summa: we have *revolted* in three ways—we have made an x into a critique of the "known world."

B

First step toward clear-mindedness: to grasp the extent to which we have been seduced—namely, it could have been exactly the other way around:

   a.   The *unknown* world could perhaps be a stupid and more trivial form of existence—so constituted as to make us long for "this world."

   b.   The *other* world, far from accommodating our desires, which would find no satisfaction there, could be among a host of things that make *this* world possible for us: coming to know it would be a way of making ourselves happy.

c. The *true* world: but who is it that tells us that the apparent world must be worth less than the true one? Doesn't our instinct contradict this judgment? Doesn't man perpetually create a fictitious world because he wants to have a world better than reality? *Above all:* why does it ever occur to us that *our* world is *not* the true one? . . . After all, the other world could be the "apparent" one (in fact, the Greeks, for example, conceived of a *realm of shadows*, an *apparent existence* alongside true existence). And finally: what gives us the right to estimate, as it were, *degrees of reality*? That's something different from an unknown world—that is already *wanting to know something of the unknown*. The "other," the "unknown," world—good! But to say "true world" means "to know something about it"—that is the *opposite* of the assumption of an x-world . . .

In summa: the world x could be in every sense more tedious, more inhuman, and less worthy than this world.

It would be something else again to assert that there are *x* worlds, i.e., every possible world besides this one. But that has *never been asserted . . .*

C

Problem: why the *notion of the other world* has always been to the disadvantage of "this" world, a criticism of it—what does that indicate?

A people proud of itself, a people in the ascendancy of life, always thinks of being *other* as being lower, being worthless; it regards the strange, the unknown world as its enemy, as its opposite; it is without curiosity, wholly dismissive of the strange . . . A people would never admit that another people were the "true people" . . .

That such a distinction is possible at all—

that one takes this world for the "apparent" one and *that* one for the "true"—is symptomatic.

The points of origin of the idea of an "other world":

- the philosopher, who invents a world of reason where *reason* and *logical* operations are adequate: this is the source of the "true" world;
- the religious man, who invents a "divine world": this is the source of the "denaturalized, counternatural" world;
- the moral man, who feigns a "free world": this is the source of the "good, perfect, just, holy" world.

What is *common* to the three points of origin: the *psychological* blunder, psychological confusions.

The "other world," as it actually appears in history, defined by what predicates? By the stig-

mata of philosophical, religious, moral prejudice.

The "other world," as it is illuminated by
these facts, as a *synonym of nonbeing*, of not
living, of not wanting to live . . .

General insight: the instinct of a *weariness
of life*, not the that of life, is what created the
"other world."

Implication: philosophy, religion, and morality are *symptoms of decadence.*

822

If my readers are sufficiently apprised of the
fact that in the grand spectacle of life even
"the good man" represents a form of *ex-
haustion*, they will respect the consistency
of Christianity, which conceives of the good
man as the *ugly* man. Christianity was right
about that.

It is unworthy of a philosopher to say, "the good and the beautiful are one"; if he goes on to say, "and also the true," one ought to thrash him. Truth is ugly.

We have *art* lest we *perish of the truth*.

8

From *Twilight of the Idols**

How the "True World" Finally
Became a Fable
HISTORY OF AN ERROR
(1888)

---

* The title (*Götzendämmerung*) is a parody of the title of Richard
Wagner's opera *Twilight of the Gods* (*Götterdämmerung*).

1. The true world attainable for the wise, the pious, the virtuous man—he lives in it, *he is it.*

    (Oldest form of the idea, relatively intelligent, convincing. Circumlocution for the proposition "I, Plato, *am* the truth.")

2. The true world, unattainable for now, but promised to the wise, the pious, the virtuous ("for the sinner who repents").

(Progress of the idea: it becomes more subtle, more insidious, more elusive—*it becomes woman*, it becomes Christian . . .)

3. The true world, unattainable, unprovable, unpromisable, and yet conceived as a consolation, an obligation, an imperative.

(The old sun in the background but seen through mist and skepticism; the idea that has become sublime, pale, Nordic, Königsbergian.*)

4. The true world—unattainable? In any case, unattained. And because unattained, also *unknown*. And consequently not consoling, redemptive, obligating: how could something unknown obligate us? . . .

(Gray morning. First yawn of reason. Cockcrow of positivism.)

5. The "true world"—an idea that is no longer

---

* Kantian. The German philosopher Immanuel Kant (1724–1804) lived in Königsberg (today Kaliningrad, Russia).

good for anything, no longer even obligating; an idea that has become useless, superfluous, *consequently* a refuted idea: let us dispense with it!

(Broad daylight; breakfast; return of *bon sens* and cheerfulness; Plato's blush; pandemonium of all free spirits.)

6. We dispensed with the true world: which world was left? The apparent one, perhaps? . . . But no! *With the true world we have also dispensed with the apparent one!*

(Midday; moment of the shortest shadow; end of the longest error; highpoint of mankind; INCIPIT ZARATHUSTRA.)

9

From *The Antichrist*
(1888)

5 9

All the work of the ancient world *in vain*: I have
no words to express my feelings about something so monstrous.— And considering that its
work was preliminary work, that the foundation for the work of millennia had just been laid
with granite self-confidence, the entire *meaning* of the ancient world in vain! . . . Wherefore

Greeks? Wherefore Romans? All preconditions for a learned culture, all scientific *methods* were there already, the great, incomparable art of reading well had already been established—that precondition for a tradition of culture, for the unity of science; natural science, in concert with mathematics and mechanics, was moving along the best paths—the *sense for facts*, the ultimate and most precious of all senses, had its schools, its already centuries-old tradition! Do we understand this? Everything *essential* for moving forward with the work had been found—the methods, it must be said ten times, *are* precisely what is essential, and most difficult, and are what have for the longest time faced the obstacles of habit and laziness. What we today have reconquered, with incomparable self-mastery—for we all somehow still have bad instincts, Christian instincts in our bones—a clear view of reality, a careful hand, patience and seriousness in the smallest matters, complete *integrity* in knowl-

edge: it was already there! Already, more than two thousand years ago! *And* in addition good, subtle tact and taste! *Not* as brain training! *Not* as "German" education with loutish manners! But as body, as gesture, as instinct—as, in a word, reality . . . *All in vain!* Overnight, just a memory!— Greeks! Romans! The refinement of instinct, of taste, methodical research, the genius for organization and administration, the faith, the *will* to a future of man, the great Yes to all things visible as an *imperium Romanum*, visible to all the senses, the grand style become not just art but reality, truth, *life* . . . And not buried overnight by natural events! Not crushed by Germanic tribes and others trampling them underfoot! But done in by sly, sneaky, invisible, anemic vampires! Not vanquished—merely sucked dry! . . . Covert vindictiveness, petty envy become *master*! Everything pathetic, suffering of itself, afflicted with bad feelings, the entire *ghetto world* of the soul *on top*, all at once!— One

need only read any Christian agitator, Saint Augustine, for example, in order to grasp, to *smell* what sort of filthy hirelings have thereby risen to the top. One would be deceiving oneself in assuming any intellectual inferiority among the leaders of the Christian movement—oh, they're smart all right, smart to the point of saintliness, these gentle church fathers! What they lack is something altogether different. Nature has neglected them—she forgot to bestow upon them a modest dowry of respectable, decent, *clean* instincts . . . Among us, there are not even men . . . Islam is right a thousand times over to despise Christianity: Islam presupposes men . . .

About the Author

FRIEDRICH NIETZSCHE (1844–1900), born near Leipzig, Prussia (now Germany), is one of the most influential and widely read thinkers of all time. He taught for ten years, from 1869 to 1879, at the University of Basel, before ill health caused him to resign his professorship and undertake an independent scholarly career. His philosophical works include *The Birth of Tragedy* (1872), *Human, All Too Human* (1878), *The Gay Science* (1882), *Thus Spoke Zarathustra* (1883), *Beyond Good and Evil* (1886), *On the Genealogy of Morals* (1887), *Twilight of the Idols* (1888), *The Antichrist* (1888), and *The Will to Power* (1883–1888).

On Truth
and Untruth

The H
Resis

In times of crisis, the great works of philosophy help us make sense of the world. The Resistance Library is a special five-book series highlighting short classic works of independent thought that illuminate the nature of TRUTH, humanity's dangerous attraction to AUTHORITARIANISM, the influence of MEDIA and MASS COMMUNICATION, and the philosophy of RESISTANCE—all critical in understanding today's politically charged world.